Guide to the Ruins

Books by Howard Nemerov

THE IMAGE AND THE LAW (POEMS)

THE MELODRAMATISTS (A NOVEL)

Guide to the Ruins

Poems by Howard Nemerov

"The living man who finds spirit, finds truth.
But if he fail, he falls among fouler shapes."

— KENA UPANISHAD

RANDOM HOUSE · NEW YORK

The author thanks the editors of the following periodicals for permission to reprint poems that have appeared in their pages: *Furioso, The Hudson Review, Harper's Bazaar, The Partisan Review, The Sewanee Review, Commentary, Halcyon, Botteghe Oscure, Here & Now, Poetry Ireland.*

To Reed Whittemore

Guide to the Ruins

One lives by commerce, said the guide.
One sells the available thing, time
And again: the ruins, the temple grove,
The gods with their noses knocked off.
One profits by the view.

It is a difficult trade, he said,
To give to the dishonored dead
Their stature and their stony eyes.
The vulgar paint has flaked away
Leaving the color of time,

The unimpassioned grey which is
Not now in commodious demand.
One gives, with broken Herakles,
A premium of legend, a pamphlet
To certify the chill.

What is it that one sells, the self?
I think not. One sells always time
Dissembled in heroic stone: such eyes
As look like cloud-reflecting lakes
In the old mountains of time.

The Contents

Guide to the Ruins

The Second-Best Bed

Consider now that Troy has burned
—Priam is dead, and Hector dead,
And great Aeneas long since turned
Away seaward with his gods
To find, found or founder, against frightful odds.

And figure to yourselves the clown
Who comes with educated word
To illustrate in mask and gown
King Priam's most illustrious son
And figure forth his figure with many another one

Of that most ceremented time
In times have been or are to be
Inhearsed in military rime;
And will recite of royal fates
Until, infamonized among those potentates

By a messenger from nearer home,
His comedy is compromised
And he must leave both Greece and Rome
Abuilding but not half begun,
To play the honest Troyan to a girl far gone.

The wench lived on, if the son died—
All Denmark wounded in one bed
Cried vengeance on the lusty bride,
Who could not care that there would follow,
After the words of Mercury, songs of Apollo.

I creature being mad
They locked me in my room,
Where, bound upon the bed
With smiling Satan there,
I would have broke my side
And given the heart to God.
Men said it was pride
Brought me to that despair.

Alas! that ever I did sin,
It is full merry in heaven.

The priest so angered me
That I would not confess.
I suffered his reproof
Scornfully, for my God
(I said) has mercy enough.
His kingdom I see
And Lucifer His rod
In my wretchedness.

Alas! that ever I did sin,
It is full merry in heaven.

When I recovered reason
I would have lived chaste,
And mocking my husband's right
I for a little season
Kept me for the sweet Christ,
Who said to me, "Dear Bride,
Rather the good man's lust
Than this dry pride."

Alas! that ever I did sin,
It is full merry in heaven.

But I, except in bed,
Wore hair-cloth next the skin,
And nursed more than my child
That grudge against my side.
Now, spirit and flesh assoil'd,
Against the wild world
I lace my pride in,
Crying out odd and even,

Alas! that ever I did sin,
It is full merry in heaven.

A Song of Degrees

Though the road lead nowhere
I have followed the road
In its blind turnings, its descents
And the long levels where the emptiness ahead
Is inescapably seen.

I have cried for justice, I have cried
For mercy, now I desire neither.
A man may grow strong in his wandering,
His foot strong as a wheel
Turning the endless road.

Foot and hand hardened to horn,
Nose but a hook of bone, and eyes
Not liquid now but stone—I
To myself violent, fiercely exult
In Zion everywhere.

The Lord might have spared us the harsh joke;
Many that live in Nineveh these days
Cannot discern their ass from a hot rock.
Perhaps the word "cattle" refers to these?

I   I went under cover of night
By back streets and alleyways,
Not as one secret and ashamed
But with a natural discretion.
I passed by a boy and a girl
Embraced against the white wall
In parts of shadow, parts of light,
But though I turned my eyes away, my mind shook
Whether with dryness or their driving blood;
And a dog howled once in a stone corner.

II Rabbi, I said,
How is a man born, being old?
From the torn sea into the world
A man may be forced only the one time
To suffer the indignation of the child,
His childish distempers and illnesses.
I would not, if I could, be born again
To suffer the miseries of the child,
The perpetual nearness to tears,
The book studied through burning eyes,
The particular malady of being always ruled
To ends he does not see or understand.

A man may be forced only the one time
To the slow perception of what is meant
That is neither final nor sufficient,
To the slow establishment of a self
Adequate to the ceremony and respect
Of other men's eyes; and to the last
Knowledge that nothing has been done,

The bitter bewilderment of his age,
A master in Israel and still a child.

III Rabbi, all things in the springtime
Flower again, but a man may not
Flower again. I regret
The sweet smell of lilacs and the new grass
And the shoots put forth of the cedar
When we are done with the long winter.

Rabbi, sorrow has mothered me
And humiliation been my father,
But neither the ways of the flesh
Nor the pride of the spirit took me,
And I am exalted in Israel
For all that I know I do not know.

Now the end of my desire is death
For my hour is almost come.
I shall not say with Sarah
That God hath made me to laugh,
Nor the new word shall not be born
Out of the dryness of my mouth.

Rabbi, let me go up from Egypt
With Moses to the wilderness of Sinai
And to the country of the old Canaan
Where, sweeter than honey, Sarah's blood
Darkens the cold cave in the field
And the wild seed of Abraham is cold.

If I forget thee, O Jerusalem . . .

Driven out of Paradise,
Shame and knowledge in their eyes,
My first parents in the dust
Taught the generations lust.

All, because Abel was slain,
Pass the narrow straits of Cain—
Children of the Land of Nod
Driven to freedom by their God.

> *The spider spun, and the gull cried:*
> *For all that, the world was wide.*

Brother against his brother fought,
Slavery was sweetly bought.
Up from Egypt then did come
All the chosen and then some.

When Saul's kingdom came to wreck
Over Agag of Amalek,
Samuel, before he died,
Made the future out of pride.

> *The spider spins, and the gull cries:*
> *Doubtless man is always wise.*

Out of pride it still is made,
Place is hollowed with the spade
For the Jew whose wicked guile
Finds no other safe exile.

Thus the planetary Jew
Bears the old law with the new,
And must suffer Israel
As stranger nations suffer hell.

The spider may spin, the gull cry:
The mighty of the earth ride high.

Virgin and Martyr

I saw the sailor dead at sea,
The soldier smashed upon the earth.
I heard the angry sergeant cry
That the fighters must go forth
Only to die. "Lord, let me too," I said,
"Lie worthless with the damaged and dead."

I saw the mad in canvas bound,
The sick, with sores biting the back,
And nurse and keeper with iron hand
Busied about the human wreck—
"Let me in turn," I prayed, "be put away
Out of the clear light and the Lord's day."

I saw old women scrub the floors
In early morning, and compared
The knees of girls in subway cars,
And I cried, "Let my knees, O Lord,
Also be broken in the marble ways,
But to Thy pleasure, Lord, pleasure and praise."

In place of pain why should I see
The sunlight on the bleeding wound?
Or hear the wounded man's outcry
Bless the Creation with bright sound?
I stretch myself on joy as on the rack,
And bear the hunch of glory on my back.

Mars

When I came from my mother's womb,
My brow already creased with doom,
I was thought a blessed child.
They tell me that I always smiled.

Blood of the Lamb
A little dram

When my teeth began to grow
That first opinion had to go.
They say my smile became a grin
And my baby lips were thin.

Smile of the ape
Biting the nape

When I showed a serious mind,
To all but study deaf and blind,
Uncles and aunts, their pride increased,
Predicted I'd become a priest.

Mouth of the lion
Singing of Sion

With these there wanted one thing more
That I might rule this threshing-floor—
Love, which does as well as hate,
Brought me to the mighty state.

Lust of the goat
And a thing of note

Honor is saved by the national will,
The burgher throws up his cap.
Gone is the soldier, over the hill,
And the rat has defended his trap.

Song

Provide your friend with almanacs
And cast him up a horoscope
Suggest the future that he lacks
Would have supplied his hopes

Give him beer and several wives
Good books and blankets for the trip
With stuff enough for fifty lives
Flatter his mortalship
Lay his weapons by his side
His address book and telephone
Try to convince him of the pride
Felt by the folks back home

And write him letters now and then
Be sure to put them in the post
Sound as cheerful as you can
Care of the holy ghost

Like anyone gone overseas
He'll take kindly to your talk
There in the camp beneath the trees
Where the sentry worms walk

The Bacterial War

Above all, not by violence—
We fought without brutality
And only test-tubes could incense
Heroes to their mortality.
The public and obedient saints,
The right to serve their single pride,
Lined up with all their documents,
Enlisted and inhaled and died.

Encounters with the enemy
Were frowned upon by adjutants;
Soldiers instead would fight to be
Strangled by simple ambience,
And breath was all the bravery
Of those without the uniform
Who did not hold Thermopylae
Against the microscopic worm.

Not guilt but total innocence
The outcome of this holy war—
Not so much man's was the offense
But it was nature's so much more.
The sons of man with perfect sense
Thereon attacked both time and space,
And sought to kill the present tense
And square the round world's grievous face.

Redeployment

They say the war is over. But water still
Comes bloody from the taps, and my pet cat
In his disorder vomits worms which crawl
Swiftly away. Maybe they leave the house.
These worms are white, and flecked with the cat's blood.

The war may be over. I know a man
Who keeps a pleasant souvenir, he keeps
A soldier's dead blue eyeballs that he found
Somewhere—hard as chalk, and blue as slate.
He clicks them in his pocket while he talks.

And now there are cockroaches in the house,
They get slightly drunk on DDT,
Are fast, hard, shifty—can be drowned but not
Without you hold them under quite some time.
People say the Mexican kind can fly.

The end of the war. I took it quietly
Enough. I tried to wash the dirt out of
My hair and from under my fingernails,
I dressed in clean white clothes and went to bed.
I heard the dust falling between the walls.

To a Friend

gone to fight for the Kuomintang

Not that, of course, you couldn't stick it out
—the cigarettes turned brown in coffee cups
And all suchlike our civil disciplines—

But that pity and hate overcame you
Where you slept in this wilderness of mind
So that wrestling, in the fixed match, seemed vain.

You be my conscience, then, and with my love
Fight what entrenched savagery you find—
Blest, if not by the angel, then by man,

Or if not by all men, yet blest of those
Who, undeceived in the strange Orient,
Would know the Harvard Club through all disguise.

But this, I see, is also vain. You know
In me a mind cancered (as you say) by
The worm I worship in the mystic rose,

Where, according to me, the blessed sit
In great humility, scratching their heads,
And pondering, according again to you,

The fathomless dialectic of the tide
But never speaking of the stinking fish
That the wave drives up but does not pull back

—*Quae mundi plaga*, dear man? China? Rome?
No matter. As between the golden mean
And the meanness of gold, there is no matter.

Or has the argument somewhere gone wrong?
Might I be forced to conclude, you to doubt?
In the violent life, you know where you are.

You have permission, then, to use my name
And die under it for all the difference—
And that's enough. I'll keep your name alive

And teach school under it, or write a book;
But when things get hard on this backward front
And all of us redeem your dollar life,

Write to me. When the engines resonate
On the cold drome, and you hear their huge strength,
The strength is not yours, neither is the will;

But write to me anyhow. Let me know,
Are there yet heroes? Do they wish to kill?
What is the will of the dead we dying do?

Grand Central, with Soldiers, in Early Morning

These secretly are going to some place,
Packing their belted, serviceable hearts.
It is the earnest wish of this command
That they may go in stealth and leave no trace,
In early morning before business starts.

A Fable of the War

The full moon is partly hidden by cloud,
The snow that fell when we came off the boat
Has stopped by now, and it is turning colder.
I pace the platform under the blue lights,
Under a frame of glass and emptiness
In a station whose name I do not know.

Suddenly, passing the known and unknown
Bowed faces of my company, the sad
And potent outfit of the armed, I see
That we are dead. By stormless Acheron
We stand easy, and the occasional moon
Strikes terribly from steel and bone alike.

Our flesh, I see, was too corruptible
For the huge work of death. Only the blind
Crater of the eye can suffer well
The midnight cold of stations in no place,
And hold the tears of pity frozen that
They will implacably reflect on war.

But I have read that God let Solomon
Stand upright, although dead, until the temple
Should be raised up, that demons forced to the work
Might not revolt before the thing was done.
And the king stood, until a little worm
Had eaten through the stick he leaned upon.

So, gentlemen—by greatcoat, cartridge belt
And helmet held together for the time—
In honorably enduring here we seek
The second death. Until the worm shall bite
To betray us, lean each man on his gun
That the great work not falter but go on.

The Hero Comes Home in His Hamper, and Is Exhibited at the World's Fair

I exhibit here the well-known failure of
Communication, nerve and power of love.
A miracle of godly medicine,
I am without facilities for sin,
Being a lump of undistinguished skin
Sans this and that after the mine went off,
Beneath my feet, with an unhealthy cough.

My flesh, a protoplastic epigram,
Suggests, without asserting, that I am;
And of my little life because I reap
The pain of waking in conclusive sleep,
I may grieve, in my basket, but not weep
Over what things, what mortal touches more,
My humble mind remaining has tears for.

Gape as you please, but keep your sympathy;
I have become my own sufficiency.
Though I was broken by the mighty fist,
By healing Nature all my wounds were kissed
And I was made the utter solipsist.
My happy state! These thoughts, within their bound,
Although they go not out, go round and round.

The Brief Journey West

By the dry road the fathers cough and spit,
This is their room. They are the ones who hung
That bloody sun upon the southern wall
And crushed the armored beetle to the floor.

The fathers' skin is seamed and dry, the map
Of that wild region where they drained the swamp
And set provision out that they might sit,
Of history the cracked precipitate,

Until the glass be shattered and the sun
Descend to burn the prosperous flesh away
Of the filthy world, so vilely fathered on
The fathers, such black cinders, sitting there.

Old pioneers, what lecheries remain?
When schoolgirls pass, what whispers of their skirts,
Cold gleams of flesh, solicit in your veined
And gemlike eyes the custom of desire?

None now. Their eyes are sunk in ancient flesh,
And the sarcastic triumph of the mind
They now enjoy, letting their lust alone
Who may have kin but have no longer kind.

Neither tomorrow's monstrous tumor nor
The reformation of the past they wish,
Who hold in silent colloquy the world
A shrivelled apple in the hand of God.

They hang at night their somber flags aloft,
And through the amorous dark pursue their theme
Of common images, that sleep may show
Them done with all disasters but the one.

Furnished and clean, this room does not betray
The traces of another tenancy,
Discourages what charges you might lay
Against its suspect calm. But lingering by
The door the woman hints a history—
The priest, your predecessor, "went away"
(So much you might have gathered; did he die?
Was it a year ago or yesterday?)

Left alone with the horrible brass bedstead,
Imagine the Father to come in at night,
Undo his collar, lie upon the bed
(His naked feet incongruously white)
And close his eyes against the icy light
For half-an-hour's nap, his dreaming head
Reworking all the daytime in a rite.
Rising, he dines on onion soup and bread.

So much you see, but cannot see his face,
And have no further wish to follow him
Where he has gone, for now the room awaits
The thud of your belongings and your name—
How easily it will encompass them!
Behind the door the sycophantic glass
Already would reflect you in a frame
That memorizes nothing but its place.

Hypocrisy! you'll get to know them well,
Wallpaper, closet, bureau and the bed,
Their repetitions in the glass, that tell
A ceaseless inventory of the bled
Stuff of your life. While in your lonely head
The poor gone priest cries vanity and hell.

O murderous usurper! Is he dead?
Has any man late heard the passing bell?

Like kings of Egypt, dreaming death a dream
In which their men and women still would come
To minister as always to a whim,
You may make of this place a kind of home:
Straighten the wrinkled window blind, make dumb
The dripping tap, let neither drop nor dram
Derange the composition of the room,
The furnished room, the garment without seam.

Fragment from Correspondence

                    . . . is superficially
The same as a hotel, grand and de luxe,
And bears its gold-encrusted coronets
On bills and menus with the usual air.

In the mornings, from the wide balconies
Where we breakfast in sunlight, I can see
The Marientor rising from silent waters,
Footed in fog but crowned with snowy light,

So arrogant and still. At ten the bus
Takes us to the baths, and calls for us again
At noon; the solemn porter tips his hat
As we pass through the doors, and we tip him.

But then, who is there whom we do not tip?
Even the chambermaids, who smooth the sheets
Our wretched bodies twisted, estimate
Exactly what our patience will endure,

And secretly I sometimes think this is
An Auschwitz for the very old and rich,
Whose money does for blood, until their blood
Leaves dry the drained purses of their flesh.

As I look up, I see the walk below,
Where Baron Kraft and Mrs Tenedine
Are walking arm in arm, her parasol
Patching a flowered shade on his parched head

—How they seem courtly, frivolous and vain!
I can't help thinking how, perhaps tonight,

Tensed on the white table stained with blood,
The Baron or the lady, like a dog

Bleeding to death in the hot New Jersey street,
Might iterate the scandal of our flesh
So loud that this firm masonry would shake
And from the cellars give its secrets up

To indignation. Though they do these things
Quietly, though I have been told nothing
Nor heard the soft tires that by night
Bear failure to the furnace and the urn,

I know these men, with their white coats, their smiles;
Their rubber and moist fingers sometimes in dreams
Press tentatively against my naked heart,
Over their masks the eyes are pitiless. . . .

The earthly doctor fiddled with his beard,
Considered the spiders Svidrigailov saw
Climbing the bath-house of eternity.
Man lives, he said, only by parricide.

Madame la Mothe had lovers one two three
Moonlit among the Dresden figurines.
And her brocaded dress was thumbed aside
Silently, and her heavy hair caressed.

The displaced persons wandered all this while
Through everglades where the loud-shrieking worm
Struggled in fragile webs; or came beyond
The tragic scene, to temples which were tombs.

The doctor, in an illustrated tome,
Saw mitred bishops creeping from a cave.
In gowns heavy with gold they went haughtily,
He thought, between the knees of Babylon.

Madame la Mothe, after the last man left,
Lifted Venetian blinds upon the town.
The lights were necklaces, and at her feet,
She thought, the world lay flat as a five-pound note.

And when she had coiled up her hair in nets
And nakedly had sunk into pale sleep,
She was as ocean, alone and deep and mute
(The moon being lost now outside the clouds).

But the doctor, with smoldering cigar,
Waked, and went patiently among the dead;

Inquired how their parents were, and when
They last had wet the bed or dreamed of God.

He read in the *Timaeus* once again
That the good old days were gone beneath the sea.
He seemed to understand, coughed once, and slept.
And then it was revealed to him in dream:

That Martin Luther shrieked aloud, Thou Pope!
And fled to England, and created the Boy Scouts,
Who were encamped above Lake Titicaca
And might invade the Rhineland if they wished.

The Old Country

Cold in cathedral the old women pray;
Outside, soldiers at ease sweat out the day.
Of Lord or Priest not much good is got
When love is cold as stone, and hate as hot.

Hate should be frozen, and most rigorous,
A soldier must be rather bone than pus;
And in the craters of his eyes must shine
The heavenly night-light of his design.

Old lovers should, that they may be well done,
Pray to be petrified by too much sun.
But such old trees are raised by burning pride
And when they fall they lie on this world's side.

All, veterans not implacable but weak,
Turn first the raw and then the roasted cheek
To the dry ice and then to the strong sun.
The God they love, the God they obey, is One.

Trial and Death, *a Double Feature*

for ALLEN TATE

A panorama of ruined houses, walls,
A broken aircraft, bundles of the dead
Lying powdered in snow. We live in our
Resentful eyes, fixed to the shifting front,
And there interpret moving shadows while
Our violated will screams from the screen.

Poor Platonists, we huddle paralyzed
To watch the black complicity of dreams
That dextrous and sinister shuffle past
So plausibly the Japanese the Jew
The housewife in Berlin, any grey face
Caught in the sunlight of a public court.

Under the automatic rifles now
They die crowded, and a good death is one
Well in the foreground and by the green flare
Given a candid gloss; photographers
May pick and choose at will, their dirty thumbs
Rifle the white eyes of the negatives.

Maybe the proper virtue of our minds
Teaches a mute respect in two dimensions
For what we might find merely base in three,
Or neutral at the least—the radar screen,
The gun, the whispering committeemen.
For even heroes have been scared of ghosts,

Those stuffed sheets that parade against a wall
And, light-struck by some weak exploding star
That catches in them radical character,

Will delegate from their dead mouths revenge
On mother or usurping uncle; so
The youngster may embrace his proper crime.

But vex not the matter with our sentiment.
Not many, ever, were five acts at dying,
Neither commanded of the Erinyes
The unbaited revengefulness, nor were
So richly by many lords and ladies danced
Attendance to anciently vulgar death,

Which if it have ten thousand several doors,
Has none of them significant of choice.
Value is something else again, as those
Know who have died for this and lived for that,
Whose languid hell exists *in vacuo*
Within the breathless center of the will.

Soon we, not violent, may go out among
The Chinese faces on the windy airdrome
Under the white sky snowing; and meanwhile
In this theater of the world's going war
We cannot but reflect their images
Who shadow blood upon our sheer cave wall.

Whether the violence dies in the idea,
Whether violence and idea die together,
Whether idea drowns in particular
Confusions, or survives in the violent man
As singular weakness and a forbidding face,
These shadow murders gain a mortal weight,

Our shrouding screen will shatter under wounds,
And horror drill the eyes in every head
So deep the dry Platonic mind must bleed.
So we attend the agon of our star
That burns, on the dusty and tarnished air,
The helpless light that is its only speech.

Sonnet

A form of Christ cut from dark wood, the pale
Paint rude on his cracked face—blood as red
As blood ran from the crown upon his head
(A hot day but cold in the cathedral,
On your own brow you felt the sweat grow cold)
To where his mouth a wound opened the sweet
Grained wood which in the forest had grown straight
Until the face was hacked out wry and old.

Where is the cup in which this blood was light
(With vinegar and sweat the natural part)?
And when the Germans bled the babies white
Where was the *skepsis* of the sculptor's art?
The question is of science not to doubt
The point of faith is that you sweat it out.

Carol

Now is the world withdrawn all
In silence and night
To beweeping Adam's fall
That this biography began
Of vile man.

Now the serpent smiles on sin
In silence and night
And sees the tumor swell within—
The heavy fruit that was the heart
Beat apart.

The spider's spittle weaves the shroud
In silence and night
Wide enough for all the proud;
Gapes the grave in pompous black
At our back.

Christ the King is born again
In silence and night
Bringing mercy to all men
Whose separate pride full is beguiled
By this child.

From Eden's Tree the Cross is made
In silence and night
Where Adam's bondman now is nailed
While the wild multitude
Cries for blood.

The great grave stone is rolled away
In silence and night
And He arose on the third day

That Adam might, free of the chains,
Choose his pains

And follow Him upon the Cross
In silence and night
And disdain all worldly loss
And to the compassionate King
Pray and sing.

Therefore do we cross this hour
In silence and night
Our grief and joy, weakness and power,
Whereto Christ's glory and His pain
Both constrain.

For there was born at Bethlehem
In silence and night
The world's and heaven's single stem
That to both kingdoms we might then
Say Amen.

Sonnet at Easter

You splice together two broomsticks, then reef
A tie (a Christmas present) at the throat.
A hat must rattle on the knob, a coat
Keep warm the chest (for he has little beef).
You set this person up disguised as you
And let him flap. He hangs lonely as grief.
His wraithless hull, no blood and no belief,
Your children don't despise but your crows do.

He is a habit now, perennial,
One of your pieties. You plant him deep,
And though you have no earthly use for him
You dress him in your father's coat, and call
Good Evening sometimes when the light is dim,
Seeing he stands for you in upright sleep.

Elegy of Last Resort

The boardwalks are empty, the cafés closed,
The bathchairs in mute squadrons face the sea.
Grey cloud goes over, the baffled involved brain
Of the old god over the vacant waters:
The proprietors of the world have gone home.

The girls, the senators, the priests, are gone,
Whose gowns the summer wind billowed no less
Than this of autumn does the scarecrow's coat;
And are not otherwise remembered than
As ideas of death in the dry sand blowing.

Aschenbach is dead, and other invalids
Have coughed their poems and died in bed.
The sea wind salts the rotting timbers,
Sand rattles against the empty windows,
Last week's newspapers crumple at the wall.

These visitors of smoke in sallow light
Curl, drift, dissolve to seaward in the wind.
They were the piteous shapes of accident
Whose winter substance ate and drank elsewhere
Time's rigors: a harder bread, more acid wine.

And some doubtless with sullen breath do praise
Autumnal pieties: the speech against
Nothing, and meaning nothing; the pain of prayer
That time's corrupted body will not hear;
The unfriendly marriage in the stranger's house.

We enter again November, and the last
Steep fall of time into the deep of time,
Atlantic and defeated, and to die

In the perplexity of a sour world
Whose mighty dispensations all are done.

This shoulder of the earth turns from the sun
Into the great darkness, into the steep
Valley of the stars, into the pit
Of frozen Cocytus, where Satan stands
Wielding the world upon his pain and pride.

We enter again November: cold late light
Glazes the field. A little fever of love,
Held in numbed hands, admires the false gods;
While lonely on this coast the sea bids us
Farewell, and the salt crust hardens toward winter.

Still Life I

The eunuch is a silly fat
Man wearing silk pajamas and
Armed with a kind of yataghan:
He guards the technicolor wives.

Within this frame, though, there are only
Three bulging oysters on a plate
Together with a white carafe
And a long loaf, all on green baize.

A marble wall and panelling
Appear behind, the marble grained
With what look like trypanosomes
Flirting in grey magnification.

Not Artemis could be more chaste
Than oysters and this alabaster
That heaves a torso from the waist;
It is cold in this public room

Of the outmoded Hotel Nord.
Even in summer icebergs float
Past where the guests sit on the porch
Knitting their sweaters too late too late.

It is as though all man had been
Castrated with a single knife.
We shudder on the porch, and hear
The foghorns weeping in the sound.

Still Life II

Dishes are apples are guitars
Floating in pools of their own flesh,
But chastity of coupled jars
Rebukes the riot of the sense.

These things upon the tilted table
Grow tense with only standing still,
While shadows patched of slate and sable
Seek to make all matter spill.

By the just rigors of an art
That hung relation on the void,
The natural man, for his poor part,
Is half-embarrassed, half-annoyed,

And in the slight migraine of form,
Holding together every side
Against the old atomic storm,
His eye grows dull, and lets things slide.

Still Life III

The décor of the darkened room
Is bleak, Victorian-ascetic.
In the scrolled and golden frame
Grey wash of light is anesthetic.

The proposition of the place,
That shadow is what light is not,
Stands abstracted on the table
By a candle and a coffee-pot,

While next to these, in grey and white
As bony as a China moon,
Are posed in agonized design
A cup, a saucer and a spoon.

Outside the cities are alight
And money talks and things make sense
And we know where we want to go
And what's to do at what expense.

Here, nothing has happened, but
Maybe to such a starving air
A young man will come in alone
And sit down in the ornate chair

And pour the coffee in the cup
To drink it though it is not hot;
Then standing, reach a careful hand
Nicely to pinch the candle out.

The Lives of Gulls and Children

Around the headland, at the end
Where they had not been before,
Paced by the white and the grey gull
With loud shrieking, and by the neat
Black-hooded tern, they found the place of death.
When they looked back along their way they saw
The footprints lonely and loud on the sand.

Few bones at first their feet kicked up,
Then more, a flat thicket of bone
And tangled cartilage, dry white and clean,
Tasting of salt when the children licked them.
Further on were feathers, then flesh
Strung on the bone ragged and rotting,
With still red tendons curled. Twice they saw
The whole delicate skeletons with the hard
Hornlike feet peacefully displayed, and there
A loud few flies buzzed on the torn meat
And dishevelled feathers; a sick and wrong
Smell mingled with the heat of the salt wind.

Silence strangely was twisted there
By the voices of the children, by
The outcries of the living gulls aloft
Swinging over the wash and rush of the sea
Between the heat of the sand and the blind sun of noon.

They saw there a great gull dying,
Huddled in the sun and shuddering out
Now and again a heavy wing in cold
Effortful motion; he stared at them
Out of a steady and majestic eye

Like a sun part baffled in cloud,
So rheumed over with the morning of death.

They would have reached out hands to him
To comfort him in that human kind
They just were learning—how anything alive,
They thought, hated loneliness most; but he,
A grim great-uncle with a cane, struck out,
Sullen and weakly fierce, with hooked beak and a claw.
He would have flown, but had not strength to rise,
Could not even, ridiculous, waddle away.

The children watched him for a moment more,
But at a distance, and did not see him die;
For he, making his death, would out-endure
What interest they had, who, being humankind,
Had homes to go to, and a bed this side of death.

But they knew the Atlantic kind he was,
And for this moment saw him swaying
In the grey dark above the cold sea miles,
Wingtips ticking the spray of the slow waves,
Leaning on the unhavening air the dangerous
Sustaining of his own breastbone; they knew
The indifference of time dragging him down.
And when after silence they turned away,
"No one has ever been here before,"
They cried, "no one, no one, no one."
Their mournful word went out, no one,
Along the shore, now that they turned for home
Bearing the lonely pride of those who die,
And paced by the sweet shrieking of the quick.

The Earthquake in the West

"At seashore resorts mothers ran
screaming down the beaches, searching
for their children, who, they feared,
might be caught up in tidal waves
that failed to materialize."

—THE NEW YORK TIMES,
THURSDAY, APRIL 14, 1949.

The art of writing an honest prose
Is no very difficult one, and may
Be mastered in little time by persons
Willing to obey such simple rules
As are to be found in almost any
Comprehensive handbook of the subject.

Beyond this, as a general thing,
One should learn to keep demeanor
In trying situations, at times
Of public crisis and disaster.
The attitude should be remote
A little, possibly a little amused;
Being a spectator requires its own
Peculiar and somewhat cold patience.

This is, admittedly, not simple.
When the familiar world shatters,
When the flat walls begin to bulge
And mothers run screaming on the shore,
It is difficult not to become
Too personally involved for the pure
And detached vision to be possible.
But then the subterranean dread
Will heave and turn in the flawed syntax
Both of the world and of the word,
Until the mothers, the children, all,
Be whelmed in the one wave together.

Praising the Poets of That Country

Many poems may be composed upon the same theme.
The differences between them may be slight
—a comma, or the tilt of an eyebrow—but not
Superficial. Whole traditions existed
For which the strict imitation of the predecessors
And not originality, was the matter of pride.
The poet then is seen as bearing a priestly part
In the ritual, confirming the continuance
Of this that and the other thing, humbly
Refreshing the hearer with his ceremony.
The place of the poet was often hereditary:
Thus, G—— was a learned man, but his grandson,
Left to himself, could not have written a line;
That was no matter. In conversation, however,
Such poets often displayed wit and extravagance
Which they would have thought unworthy
Of the strenuous character of their art.
It was not, that is, a question of "talent,"
But rather of a fanatic and ascetic practice
Of willed submission to the poem existing.
R——'s epitaph read, "The man who placed
The adjective 'calm' in its proper context."
This, a matter of pride, in forty years of work.

Then the beloved face was known to the whole people.
The complexion *white,* the eyes *dark,* and *like
Twin suns,* the lips *like cherries* or
Of the color of rubies, the hair *glorious
And shiningmost mystery,* the shoulders *like cream*
And then the Sestos and the Abydos of it.
These things were well-known, and each man with his doxy
Might make what he might out of the whole business
Nightlong, and daylong if he liked and was able.

Under the cadence the beat of the common meter
Sustained the matter, and the exact rime
Measured the moment with a considered force.

These not eccentric men were held in honor
Wilder than the expectations of despair;
No valorous excess could mar those characters
That guarded times to time on the baffled drum,
Holding in secret the still-beating victim heart,
While elsewhere the profane crowds would walk
Unthinking their free and many ways to death.

Madrigal

She is the darkness where I wander
Who was the light that found my way.
What time and choice have torn asunder
Come together in no day.

Blackness her great beauty bringeth
Upon me, and I go my way
Singing as one lonely, that singeth
Unregarding and astray.

Night time on her also is fallen,
Shadow clouds her perfect way.
For her the winter sun rides sullen
And shines not on the dark day.

To such a year no springtime riseth,
Nor is no excellence in May,
But darkness in the sky abideth
Where the world wanders astray.

Four Sonnets

1.

Earth orbits on the sun and has no sign
But her fidelity must be her ruin,
Yet serpentwise on the consuming line
She flies from darkness into noon
Seeking to burn; while on the shadow side
Where dreams are plotted at the speed of light
The brain-cold sleepers lie in lonesome pride
Staring with glacial and ecstatic sight.
I circle so, contracted to your sun
Which reins me, though my wintry mind's desire
Elsewhere would spend that force by which I run
Through death to landfall in your centrique fire;
  Only to show what quality of lust
  Enters the composition of this dust.

2.

You too will cool, though from your distance light
Cold and denatured still may seem to flow
Which space not yet annihilates, nor night
Proves a divorce, and mortuary show.
The imposition of your eye's regard
Even in cause of death deceives me still
After that love that lived without reward
Is burnt aether to earth despite your will.
Yet you in your own deceit own coldness kills,
And when your latest light is in my eyes
Drowned and entombed, when by disordered wheels
Beyond the sun you wander through blind skies,

Remember him your fire chilled with fever
Sometimes to shake him, but to warm him never.

3.

Of fire and of lust proceeds the world
And not of your cold liking, nor the chaste
Glass to your mind, the moon aged and scarred
By the huge and master light in which you waste.
Scanning your distant heaven I may see
Your too nebulous light but not your flame,
Not sacred rage but pale astronomy
Still spinsterish with a too ancient fame.
Think, if the sun should waste in your delay
And sink down bleeding from the bloodied sky,
Your pale reflexion, at his final day,
Ends with his lustiness, and you must die.
 Then thinking of that outer night you know
 This darkness where you make me wander now.

4.

Your beauty once the profit of your scorn
Blinded almost the burning eye of time,
Which from the head of heaven being torn
Had left the world lit by your lonely prime;
But having burned your days to brilliant light,
Feeding expression on your own cold blood,
The waste of this is reckoned up to night
And that you cannot keep which kept you proud.
So to the blackness of an unloved day
Your mortal flare condemns the world and you,
Which locked in mutual contempt display
The scars of married rage, bound to be true
 With neither love nor pride nor beauty won
 From your proud pacing of the lonely sun.

The Ecstasies of Dialectic

Her laughter was infectious; so, some found,
Her love. Several young men reasonably
Regret inciting her to gratitude
And learning of her ardent facility.

She has gone, back it may be to the world,
To ply her silken exercise elsewhere.
Now is occasion for the medication
(As possible) of ills not all of the heart,

And certain hints, conveyed in sermon or
By private word, are reasoning the weight
Of pleasures, pains. Thus her capable joys
Are debased by her ignominious communications.

"The flesh, the rouged cheekbones of Babylon,
The unclean loins, the thief of legal delight,
O ye generations!" "The spider that eats up
Her mate!" "The test-tube of iniquity!"

Despite the wisdom of Christian Epicures
Many of the affected more regret
Her going than her legacy. They huddle
At street corners, before drugstores, and moon

Over the hour of pestilent delight,
The yellow taste good times will always have.
"The proof of the apple is in the worm," they say,
And hug their new knowledge of life and death.

I Under the moon my brother's body lay,
Beyond the city, on the vacant plain,
In the pale light his face untimely grey
With blowing dust over the dry bloodstain.

Keeping the intervals of Creon's guard
I scratched the shallow grave, and buried him
With my own hands bloodied on the hard
Clay soil. His cold eyes for the last time

Stared up, as though he tried to lift his head
And speak through choking death, or his cold hand
To touch my shoulder and so to his poor bed
Beckon me down. And as I understand,

No form or ceremony of the state
So drew me, breathless, to my brother's side,
But my blind will, having all life in hate,
Gave me to kingly death to be his bride.

II There followed capture; tears, threats, high talk
By both parties, myself as obstinate
As Creon could be; neither one would balk
At the last fence whether of will or fate.

For I desired the locked and choking tomb
Which all my light desires had but veiled.
Deathward dreaming, the mind wants little room,
Its own room in darkness, and that room sealed.

I know now that it had to be this way
Always (and the young Haemon too is dead).
The bride is dressed and goes forth from the day
To the dark hour of her desire and dread.

Sonnet

"The one complete book for serious players . . . how to be
a consistent winner . . . full information on all forms of
cheating . . . how to avoid being a 'sucker' . . . the all-
inclusive guidebook for all who play for money."
　　　　　　　　　　　　　　　　　　　　—ADVERTISEMENT.

It seems to be the trouble, everyone
Is not the one always who wins, though he
Be never so serious, and never see
On next to nothing only for the fun.
Maybe no guide, when the great wheel is spun,
Can balance man against peripety,
Or keep him upright that he may not be
By forms of cheating done if not undone.

It is a sin against the life to come
If Mistress Fortune falsely implicate
Equality and grace, for wise or dumb
They win not always in their playing state,
　　　　But suckers and the guileless, at this game,
　　　　Come out as well, or so some guidebooks claim.

A Lean and Hungry Look

It is cold in my refrigerator.
Salami, liverwurst and beef
Are frozen there and frozen well,
With pickled herring, lettuce leaf
And consommé I left to jell.

It is warm in my refrigerator.
Steady blue flame, to my belief,
Signifies that I live well—
Incessant whining is the chief
Complaint I have about my cell.

It tells me my refrigerator
Suffers the European grief,
Its stout heart's oily tears expel
Remorse but offer no relief,
Freezing the hard eyeballs of hell.

The Phoenix

The Phoenix comes of flame and dust
He bundles up his sire in myrrh
A solar and unholy lust
Makes a cradle of his bier

In the City of the Sun
He dies and rises all divine
There is never more than one
Genuine

By incest, murder, suicide
Survives the sacred purple bird
Himself his father, son and bride
And his own Word